MW00475327

Timeless Seeds of Advice

*

The Sayings of Prophet Muhammad ﷺ, Ibn Taymiyyah, Ibn al-Qayyim, Ibn al-Jawzi and Other Prominent Scholars in Bringing Comfort and Hope to the Soul

B. B. Abdulla

2019

Copyright © 2018 B. B. Abdulla

All rights reserved. No part of this publication may be reproduced, stored in a retrieval system, or transmitted, in any form or by any means for commercial purposes without prior permission of the author. The author affirms the readers' right to share this book for personal, non-commercial purposes.

Dedication

All praise and gratitude are due to Allah ﷻ. May Allah's peace and blessings be on Muhammad ﷺ, on his family and on his companions.

This book is dedicated to those who feel an emptiness, sadness, loss of hope or distance from Allah ﷻ. May Allah ﷻ guide you by the way of these reminders and heart softeners to better yourself and rise above the cloud that is covering your heart.

وَذَكِّرْ فَإِنَّ ٱلذِّكْرَىٰ تَنفَعُ ٱلْمُؤْمِنِينَ

"And go on reminding [people], it is good for those who believe to be reminded." [Quran 51:55]

This page intentionally left blank.

Preface

I have taken these sayings with me and carried them in my heart. They have lent me great strength and hope throughout the years. I wanted to compile them into a book so as to benefit the wider community Insha'Allah (God-willing). I am only a servant in need of mercy.

Whoever desires goodness, then let him take account of himself and reproach himself day and night in self-development. Nothing is more beneficial than reflecting upon the Quran which is a love letter composed to you from Allah ﷻ Himself.

The root of happiness in this world is contentment. By being content, you are led to the doors of gratefulness. By being content, you are patient and satisfied with the decrees of your Master, Allah ﷻ. By being grateful, you take that a step further and are not only content, but happy, and grateful for the state you are in. As for the reward of the patient ones, Allah ﷻ says: "Say, '[God says], believing servants, be mindful of your Lord! Those who do good in this world will have a good reward– God's earth is *wide*—and those who persevere patiently will be given a full and unstinting reward.'" [Quran 39:10]

— A servant in need of Allah's mercy

Hope

In *sujūd* (prostration), I found my home

1

Ibn al-Qayyim رحمه الله (may Allah have mercy on him) said: "Shaykh al-Islām Ibn Taymiyyah[1], may Allah ﷻ honor his soul and illuminate his grave, once said to me..." (explaining with a metaphorical example the purpose of seeking refuge in Allah ﷻ from Satan):

"If the shepherd's dog ever barks at you attempting to attack you, then do not engage it in a fight. Instead, turn to the shepherd and seek his help for he will leash it and save you the trouble."[2]

When a person takes refuge in Allah ﷻ from the accursed Satan, He protects him and keeps away Satan's harm and evil from reaching him.

---

[1] Ibn Taymiyyah's name is controversial today due to the use (and abuse) of his thought by militant groups. The late Harvard scholar Shahab Ahmed and the Belgian scholar Yahya Michot are two scholars who have worked hard to re-analyze Ibn Taymiyyah's massive corpus in order to discover the "real" Ibn Taymiyyah. Their results suggest that Ibn Taymiyyah was a far more sophisticated and balanced thinker than his extremist admirers realize. See Shahab Ahmed and Yossef Rapoport, *Ibn Taymiyya and His Times*, Karachi: Oxford University Press, 2017; Yahya Michot, *Ibn Taymiyya: Against Extremisms*, Beirut: Dar Albouraq, 2012.
[2] Ibn al-Qayyim, *Inner Dimensions of the Prayer*.

2

Abū Bakr al-Ṣiddīq رضي الله عنه (may Allah be pleased with him) said: "I wish I were a hair in the side of a believing servant."[1]

He رضي الله عنه expressed the extent of his fear of Allah ﷻ and how he would do anything to please his Master. He رضي الله عنه used to weep and say: "cry and if you cannot, try hard to."

To this effect, Ibn al-Jawzi رحمه الله said: "When true fear of God is realized in your heart, all good things will come to you."[2]

---

[1] Ibn al-Qayyim, *Inner Dimensions of the Prayer*. Recorded by Imam Aḥmad.
[2] Ikram Hawramani, *The Sayings of Ibn al-Jawzi*.

3

My God, and my Lord, who do I have besides You?

In life, we are taught time and again that in blessing and in hardship the only one who can fully comprehend our situation is Allah ﷻ. The ultimate help is from Allah. Striving to gain the acceptance and love of Allah ﷻ will inevitably lead to an escape out of every difficult and misery one experiences in life.

"Anyone who believes in God and the Last Day should heed this: God will find a way out for those who are mindful of Him, and will provide for them from an unexpected source; God will be enough for those who put their trust in Him. God achieves His purpose; God has set a due measure for everything." [Quran 65:2-3]

These words remind us that besides Allah ﷻ we have no one to aid us. Allah's ﷻ help is near and the believers will be victorious by the will of Allah. Despair not; Allah ﷻ will never leave the one He loves out in the dark. Imagine for a moment what you would do for someone you love if they are distressed or sad. It is incomparable on any level to the help and support that will be received from Allah ﷻ. Allah's ﷻ timing and knowledge are far beyond ours to comprehend the delaying of ease or the answer to a supplication.

Ibn al-Jawzi رحمه الله to this effect remarked: "If you repent and supplicate but are not answered, reflect on your condition, for perhaps your repentance has not been realized, therefore work toward completing it. Then supplicate, and do not tire of supplication, for perhaps it is in your best interest for the answer to be delayed, or for it not to be answered. In this way you accumulate rewards, and you will be answered through that which benefits you, and perhaps it is to your benefit that you do not get what you seek, but are given something better that replaces it."[1]

Ultimately for a true believer it comes down to: God is enough for us: He is the best protector.

---

[1] Ikram Hawramani, *The Sayings of Ibn al-Jawzi*.

4

"He is with you wherever you may be." [Quran 57:4]

The words of Allah ﷻ are tranquility to the hearts of the believers and those who reflect upon the Quran. Knowing that Allah ﷻ is with us in our affairs at all times is one of the greatest blessings a servant can have in their lifetime. For the one who is deprived of Allah ﷻ is deprived of all good; while the one who has Allah ﷻ has gained all goodness. Allah has infinite knowledge of our affairs. Knowing this should bring joy and happiness to our hearts. "He has the keys to the Unseen: no one knows them but Him. He knows all that is in the land and sea. No leaf falls without His knowledge, nor is there a single grain in the darkness of the earth, or anything, fresh or withered, that is not written in a clear Record." [Quran 6:59]

5

Shaykh Ibn Taymiyyah[1] رحمه الله said: "Verily, I constantly renew my Islam until this very day, as up to now, I do not consider myself to have ever been a good Muslim."

While Shaykh Ibn Taymiyyah رحمه الله is by far one of the greatest scholars, yet his humble nature and fear of Allah ﷻ are depicted here. One should never depend on their past deeds and should continuously strive to better themselves spiritually and to nourish their souls. In having a humble nature, he was able to better himself rather than stuck in one position or worse yet reverse.

Allah ﷻ says: "Do not strut arrogantly about the earth: you cannot break it open, nor match the mountains in height." [Quran 17:37]

---

[1] Mentioned by Ibn Qayyim al-Jawziyyah.

6

Ramadan shows us our potential and what we can be if we wanted.

Despite the short amount of time, we achieve so much in spirituality and self-development. This not only illustrates for us how we can be productive if we manage our time efficiently but that what we often think to be impossible is possible. Patience is the key to the greatest of achievements. The Prophet ﷺ left Makkah with nothing in 620 AH, yet returned in 630 AH to peacefully become the master of the city. It only took 10 years of patience and hard work to achieve one of the greatest achievements–liberating the house of Allah ﷻ from the idols.

It was said: "How do we observe patience?"

"In the same manner that we fast; completely certain that the *adhān* of Maghrib will eventually be called."

Ibn al-Qayyim[1] رحمه الله says: "Patience is for the heart to not feel anger towards that which is destined and for the mouth to not not complain."

"Don't let your definition of success, failure or self-worth be anything other than your position with Him. And if you do this, you become unbreakable, because your handhold is unbreakable. You become unconquerable because your supporter can never be conquered. And you will never become empty because your source of fulfillment is unending and never diminishes."[2]

The Prophet ﷺ says: "The eye weeps and the heart grieves, but we say only what our Lord is pleased with."[3]

---

[1] *Al-'Uddah*, p.156.
[2] Yasmin Mogahed.
[3] Sunan Abī Dawūd 3126.

7

Ali Bannat[1] on being asked about his biggest regret: "My biggest regret is that it took a man in suit to tell me that I am going to die, but Allah told me all my life and I did not believe him"

Ibn al-Jawzi رحمه الله says: "The ship of your lifetime is approaching the coast of the graveyard. What is the matter with you that you are busy inside the ship trying to acquire goods?"[2]

ʿAlī رضي الله عنه said: "The Hereafter is traveling towards us, and this life is traveling away from us, so be from the children of the Hereafter and not from the children of this world. For today is action without reckoning, and tomorrow is reckoning without action."

---

[1] Ali Bannat (1982-2018): Muslim Australian businessman and philanthropist.

[2] Ikram Hawramani, *The Sayings of Ibn al-Jawzi*.

8

ʿAbdullāh b. ʿUmar رضي الله عنه said, "Allah's Messenger ﷺ took hold of my shoulder and said, 'Be in this world as if you were a stranger or a traveler.'" The sub-narrator added: Ibn ʿUmar used to say, "If you survive till the evening, do not expect to be alive in the morning, and if you survive till the morning, do not expect to be alive in the evening, and take from your health for your sickness, and (take) from your life for your death."[1]

"O friend, the cloth from which your burial shroud will be cut may have already reached the market and yet you remain unaware."[2]

---

[1] Ṣaḥīḥ al-Bukhārī 6416.
[2] Imam al-Ghazali.

9

On the authority of Abū Hurayra رضي الله عنه, who said that the Prophet ﷺ said:

"Allah the Almighty said: I am as My servant thinks I am, I am with him when he makes mention of Me. If he makes mention of Me to himself, I make mention of him to Myself; and if he makes mention of Me in an assembly, I make mention of him in an assembly better than it. And if he draws near to Me an arm's length, I draw near to him a cubit, and if he draws near to Me a cubit, I draw near to him a fathom. And if he comes to Me walking, I go to him at speed."[1]

Ibn al-Qayyim رحمه الله also said: "The more you have good expectations of your Lord and hope in Him, the more you will rely on and trust in Him. This is why some explained true reliance and trust to be having good expectations of Allah. In reality, having good expectations of Him leads to relying on and trusting in Him, as it is unthinkable that one can

[1] Related by al-Bukhārī (7405), Muslim (2675 a), al-Tirmidhī (3603) and Ibn Māja (3822).

trust in someone that he has bad expectations of or no hope in, and Allah knows best."[1]

Abū Hurayra رضي الله عنه reported:

Allah Most High says: "He who is hostile to a friend of Mine I declare war against. My servant approaches Me with nothing more beloved to Me than what I have made obligatory upon him, and My servant keeps drawing nearer to Me with voluntary works until I love him. And when I love him, I am his hearing with which he hears, his sight with which he sees, his hand with which he seizes, and his foot with which he walks. If he asks me, I will surely give to him, and if he seeks refuge in Me, I will surely protect him."[2]

Hearing these beautiful words of Allah through our beloved messenger brings tranquility and hope back to our hearts and shatters the possibility of sadness ever engulfing our hearts. Internalizing these words will not only revive your heart but allow you to rise spiritually.

---

[1] *Tahdhīb Madārij al-Sālikīn.*

[2] Related by al-Bukhārī (6502), Aḥmad b. Ḥanbal, al-Bayhaqī and others.

10

"And the hereafter is better for you than the first (life)." [Quran 93:4]

"Sin is inevitable

Imān fluctuates

Your Allah loves to forgive.

We walk away often. It is important to always return to Him–regardless of how many times we leave or how far we go.

Turn back because you are welcome.

Turn back, no matter how small the steps you take seem to be.

Turn back

because He will always be patient with you, even if you are impatient with yourself."[1]

---

[1] Samihah Pargas.

11

He is breaking you to heal you.

Ibn al-Qayyim رحمه الله said: "From the perfection of Allah's *iḥsān* (excellence and bounty) is that He allows His servant to taste the bitterness of the break before the sweetness of the mend. He does not break His believing servant except to mend him. And He does not withhold from him except to give to him. And He does not test him (with hardship), except to cure him."

Allah ﷻ says: "if you are grateful, I will give you more and more." [Quran 14:7]

Ibn al-Qayyim رحمه الله also said: "There is no joy for the one who does not bear sadness, there is no sweetness for the one who does not have patience, there is no delight for the one who does not suffer and there is no relaxation for the one who does not endure fatigue."

Allah ﷻ says in His Book: "Do not lose hope nor be sad." [Quran 3:139]

"And your Lord is going to give you, and you will be satisfied." [Quran 93:5]

"Is Allah not enough for His servant?" [Quran 39:36]

Ibn al-Qayyim writes: "He who has tested the servant is the Most Wise, the Most Merciful and He did not test him with the affliction to destroy, punish or overwhelm him. Rather, the affliction is merely a test of his patience, his contentment with Allah and his faith. In addition, Allah wants to hear the servant's pleas, supplications and humility before Him, his seeking refuge with Him, his heart's humility before Him and his explaining his sadness to Him (alone)."[1]

---

[1] Ibn al-Qayyim, *The Prophetic Medicine.*

12

Ibn ʿUmar رضي الله عنه reported:

The Prophet ﷺ said, "The most beloved people to Allah are those who are most beneficial to the people. The most beloved deed to Allah is to make a Muslim happy, or to remove one of his troubles, or to forgive his debt, or to feed his hunger. That I walk with a brother regarding a need is more beloved to me than that I seclude myself in this mosque in Medina for a month. Whoever swallows his anger, then Allah will conceal his faults. Whoever suppresses his rage, even though he could fulfill his anger if he wished, then Allah will secure his heart on the Day of Resurrection. Whoever walks with his brother regarding a need until he secures it for him, then Allah the Exalted will make his footing firm across the bridge on the day when the footings are shaken."[1]

[1] *Al-Muʿjam al-Awsaṭ* 6192; graded *ṣaḥīḥ* by Al-Albānī.

13

The Prophet ﷺ said: "The most truthful word said by a poet is that of Labīd: 'Indeed, everything else besides Allah is false and vain…'"[1]

Shaykh Muḥammad b. al-Mukhtār al-Shanqīṭī رحمه الله said: "Don't assume bad of Allah, for by Allah, if you obey Him, He will make for you a source of relief and a way out, and if you are alone within your family and society, then Allah will accompany you in your loneliness. And He will strengthen your heart, and make it firm with His guidance."

"He will give you (something) better than what was taken from you." [Quran 8:70]

---

[1] Sahih Muslim 2256 a.

14

Allah gives from His goodness.

Shaykh al-Islām Ibn Taymiyyah رحمه الله said: "Whoever exerts himself and seeks aid from Allah and adheres to seeking forgiveness and sacrificing, then most definitely Allah will give him from His goodness that which had never crossed his mind."[1]

"Say, '[God says], believing servants, be mindful of your Lord! Those who do good in this world will have a good reward– God's earth is *wide*–and those who persevere patiently will be given a full and unstinting reward.'" [Quran 39:10]

---

[1] *Majmūʿ al-Fatāwā* 5/62.

15

"It is not true that if we had true faith we would not be sad. Prophets (may Allah's peace be upon them all), and righteous people experienced a great deal of sadness. The Quran is full of stories in which the central theme is sadness. Sadness is a reality of life. The Quran is not there to eliminate sadness, but to navigate it. Sadness is one of the tests of life, just as happiness, and anger are tests."[1]

Every single success you experience is a combination of two things: your effort and Allah's help. When you do not put in enough effort, Allah does not give His *baraka* (blessing). And sometimes you might put in a lot of effort, but you may not see the result you expected. That, also, is Allah's *baraka*.

When calamity hits, we start feeling like Allah owes us something. Allah owes us nothing. We owe Allah everything. So what if this life isn't perfect? It is not Jannah.

May Allah not allow our hearts to become hardened, may Allah ﷻ make us a people sincerely of remembrance to Allah, may Allah grant us the

[1] Nouman Ali Khan.

gift of better company than ourselves that keeps our egos in check. May Allah give us the ability to give advice to those around us. The people of *lā ilāha illallāh* are more beloved to us, are closer to us than even the bond of blood. *Lā ilāha illallāh* brings us closer than the bond of blood. And may Allah ﷻ make us share that love and affection and unity with the other Muslims and show them that sincerity from the bottom of our hearts. May Allah ﷻ penetrate good advice into the heart of those who need it, may Allah ﷻ make us capable of taking advice and taking the best of it and not allowing advice to become a means by which our egos are inflated. May Allah ﷻ keep us humble before Him, forgive our shortcomings that have occurred in the past, and may He ﷻ make us of those whose hearts are perpetually being cleansed.

You know what the Quran teaches me? The Quran teaches me that an incredibly wealthy man can be a failure (Pharaoh) and a homeless man can be successful (Prophet Ibrāhīm عليه السلام). It teaches me that success has nothing to do with wealth and failure has nothing to do with poverty.

16

If they ask you: "Why are you sad?" Tell them truthfully, and say to them:

I rarely make *istighfār* (asking Allah ﷻ for forgiveness) and I left reading the Quran.

Ibn Taymiyyah رحمه الله said: "The strength of the heart returns when one repents!"[1]

May Allah ﷻ make us of people who constantly make *istighfār* and read the Quran with contemplation.

[1] *Diseases of the Heart and their Cures*, p. 56.

17

“For the people that are out there that are sick or worried or stressed, I always say to you people, don’t worry. Allah will send you people that you never expected. If you really need someone, you just have to trust Allah and have *tawakkul* (trust and reliance) in Allah.”[1]

[1] Ali Bannat.

18

Abu Dharr رضي الله عنه reported:

Messenger of Allah ﷺ said, "I see what you do not see, and I hear what you do not hear; heaven has squeaked, and it has right to do so. By Him, in Whose Hand my soul is, there is not a space of four fingers in which there is not an angel who is prostrating his forehead before Allah, the Exalted. By Allah, if you knew what I know, you would laugh little, weep much, and you would not enjoy women in beds, but would go out to the open space beseeching Allah."[1]

'Uthmān b. 'Affān رضي الله عنه, said: "Do not forget the angel of death, for he does not forget you..."[2]

"If you knew what you are facing after death, you would not eat your meal nor drink with any appetite... I wish I were a tree to be bitten (by insects) and then eaten."[3]

---

[1] Ibn Māja Vol. 5, Book 37, Hadith 4190. Graded *ḥasan*.
[2] *Al-Mujālasa wa-Jawāhir al-'Ilm*, vol. 2, p. 73.
[3] Ibn Qayyim al-Jawziyyah, *Spiritual Diseases and their Cures*.

19

Al-Ḥasan al-Baṣrī رحمه الله said,

"Indeed, those who came before you saw the Quran as personal letters from their Lord. So they would ponder over it by night and yearn for it by day."[1]

"The Quran is not only a book of guidance; Allah wrote us a 632-page love letter."[2]

---

[1] Imam al-Nawawī, *Al-Tibyān fī Ādāb Ḥamalat al-Qur'ān.*
[2] Wisam Sharieff.

20

"But Allah is your protector, and He is the best of helpers." [Quran 3:150]

How calming an effect these words have on the soul of a believer knowing that Allah ﷻ, the Lord of the worlds, is there for you with all His power and might.

21

"If the human knew the pleasure of meeting Allah and being near Him, he would feel grief for being distant from Him."[1]

For everything you lose there is a replacement but for Allah ﷻ; if you lose Him there is no replacement.

The main connection between us and Allah ﷻ is the *ṣalāh* (daily prayers). Each *ṣalāh* not only renews our pledge as servants of Allah ﷻ the Almighty but it establishes our direct connection to Allah ﷻ. To this effect, ʿUmar b. al-Khaṭṭāb رضي الله عنه said: "Hold onto your *ṣalāh* because if you lose that, you will lose everything else."[2] Thus as Yasir Qadhi says: "if you ever find yourself rushing through salat (prayer) to make it to another engagement, it is time to reorganize your priorities."

---

[1] Ibn al-Qayyim, *Al-Fawā'id*, p. 119.
[2] Ibn ʿAbd al-Barr, *al-Istidhkār*, Kitāb al-Ṭahāra.

22

Allah ﷻ mentions His book: "and Allah would not punish them while they seek forgiveness." [Quran 8:33]

Shaykh al-Islām Ibn Taymiyyah رحمه الله said:

"Allah has informed us that He will not punish those who (sincerely) seek forgiveness (for their sins); that is because seeking forgiveness wipes away the sin, which is the reason for being punished, therefore (seeking forgiveness) repels the punishment."

23

Abū Yazīd رحمه الله said: "I continued dragging my soul to Allah whilst it cried, until it finally surrendered itself and came with me to Allah smiling."[1]

Imam al-Shāfiʿī رحمه الله said: "To be able to thank Allah for a blessing is a blessing within itself."[2]

---

[1] Ibn al-Qayyim, *Badāʾiʿ al-Fawāʾid*.
[2] Imam al-Shāfiʿī, *al-Risāla*.

24

A man came to al-Ḥasan al-Baṣrī رحمه الله and said: "O Abū Sa'īd, I complain to you of the hardness of my heart!"

Al-Ḥasan رحمه الله said: "Discipline it with *dhikr*."[1]

"Those who have faith and whose hearts find peace in the remembrance of God– truly it is in the remembrance of God that hearts find peace– those who believe and do righteous deeds: joy awaits these, and their final homecoming will be excellent." [Quran 13:28-29]

---

[1] Ibn al-Qayyim, *al-Wābil al-Ṣayyib*.

25

The most beautiful thing is that He knows what you are about to tell Him and yet He still listens.

This is beautifully illustrated from Mūsā's story عليه السلام.

Allah ﷻ says: "Mūsā, what is that in your right hand?" [Quran 20:17]

Mūsā عليه السلام him replies: "It is my staff,' he said, 'I lean on it; restrain my sheep with it; I also have other uses for it." [Quran 20:18]

Allah ﷻ, despite knowing it is a staff, still asks and wants to hear His servant's voice and reply. Although Allah ﷻ knows what is bothering you and what your problems are, He wants you to talk to Him, through the believer's most powerful weapon: *dua*.

26

Luqmān عليه السلام said to his son: "O my beloved son, do not delay repentance for indeed punishment can come unexpectedly."[1]

Ibn al-Qayyim رحمه الله said: "Do not belittle a small sin, for the biggest of fires can be caused by the smallest of sparks."

---

[1] Imam al-Bayhaqī, *Shuʿab al-Īmān* 6701.

27

Shaykh al-Islām Ibn Taymiyyah رحمه الله said: "Remembrance of Allah for the heart is like water for the fish; and what will be the state of the fish when it is separated from water?"

"Is there anyone who has achieved closeness to God and not found that with Him is everything that they need and desire?"[1]

---

[1] Ikram Hawramani, *The Sayings of Ibn al-Jawzi*.

28

"O you, the sins you commit shall never affect your lord; He only wants to keep you (away) from (your own) harm. You should know that your obedience to Him shall never fetch Him any benefit; your obedience is only for your own benefit. So, contemplate your situation."[1]

---

[1] Ibn al-Jawzi, *Kitāb al-Laṭā'if fī-l-Wa'ẓ.*

29

Al-Ḥasan al-Baṣrī رحمه الله said: "Sell this life for the next and you win both of them. Sell the next life for this and you lose both of them."[1]

Mālik b. Dīnar رحمه الله said: "Whoever proposed to the world should know that the world would not be satisfied until he gives up all of his *dīn* as dowry."

Abū Hurayra رضي الله عنه reported that the Prophet ﷺ said, "A place in Paradise as small as a bow is better than all that on which the sun rises and sets."[2]

He also said, "A single endeavor in Allah's Cause in the afternoon or in the forenoon is better than all that on which the sun rises and sets."[3]

---

[1] *Al-Ḥilya* 2/143.
[2] Ṣaḥīḥ al-Bukhārī 2793.
[3] Ṣaḥīḥ al-Bukhārī 2792.

30

Abū Hurayra رضي الله عنه reported that the Messenger of Allah ﷺ said: "Richness does not lie in the abundance of (worldly) goods but richness is the richness of the soul (heart, self)."[1]

The richness of the soul emanates from the worship of Allah alone and in following the Sunna of the Prophet ﷺ. The good deeds one performs are likened to a tree in the Quran: "[Prophet], do you not see how God makes comparisons? A good word is like a good tree whose root is firm and whose branches are high in the sky, yielding constant fruit by its Lord's leave– God makes such comparisons for people so that they may reflect" [14: 24-25]

"Goodly word refers to testifying to *lā ilāha ilallāh,* (none has the right to be worshipped but Allah), while goodly tree is a believer (whose root is firmly fixed), indicates that *lā ilāha ilallāh,* (none has the right to be worshipped but Allah) is firm in the believers' heart. The branches refer to the believer

---

[1] Ṣaḥīḥ Muslim 1051.

whose good works ascend to heaven by day and by night and at all times."[1]

The saying goes: "O Allah, I never knew heartbreak until I disobeyed You and I never knew happiness until I obeyed You."

[1] Ibn Kathīr.

31

Imam al-Shāfiʿī رحمه الله said: "All humans are dead except those who have knowledge; and all those who have knowledge are asleep, except those who do good deeds; and those who do deeds are deceived, except those who are sincere; and those who are sincere are always in a state of worry."

Sufyān al-Thawrī 's mother رحمه الله used to say to him: "My son, do not seek knowledge unless you intended to act upon it. Otherwise, it will be a calamity upon you on the Day of Rising."[1]

May Allah ﷻ grant us sincerity, and the ability to act upon knowledge in doing good.

[1] ʿAbd al-ʿAzīz Sayyid al-Ahl, *al-Imām al-Awzāʿī Faqīh Ahl al-Shām.*

32

Al-Ḥasan al-Baṣrī رحمه الله said: "As much as you fix your *ṣalāh*, your life will be fixed. If you are wondering why there is a delay in your sustenance, in your marriage, in your work, in your health, look into your *ṣalāh*; are you delaying it?"

Ibn al-Qayyim رحمه الله said: "You stand in your prayers with your body, directing your face to the *qibla*, while your heart is directed to a different territory? Woe to you! That prayer (of yours) is not worthy of being a *mahr* (dower) for paradise, how then can it be befitting for (attaining) the love of Allah?"[1]

---

[1] *Badāʾiʿ al-Fawāʾid.*

33

"You must stop your fingers from grabbing the water when the river, much like your fate, leads its own way."

"And unto Allah is the end of all affairs." [Quran 31:22]

Someone asked al-Ḥasan al-Baṣrī رحمه الله: "What is the secret to your piety?"

He replied: "I understood four things:

1. I understood that my *rizq* (provision/sustenance decreed by Allah ﷻ) cannot be taken by anyone, so my heart become content.
2. I understood that no one can do my actions (worship) for me, so I started doing them myself.
3. I understood that Allah is watching me, so I became ashamed to do wrong.
4. I understood that death is waiting for me, so I started to prepare for my meeting with Allah"

May Allah ﷻ grant us this understanding and the ability to act according to it.

34

One wise man said: "Why do you worry? For Allah ﷻ provides for the ant in the dark hole and the fishes in the depth of the oceans. Do you then think that He will forget you?"

"When those few young men took refuge in the cave, they said, 'our Lord! Have a special mercy and guide us to rationality in our matter'." [Quran 18:10]

That is a supplication that exemplifies depending on Allah ﷻ and knowing that Allah will provide for you with firm conviction. It was the conviction of the "people of the cave" that saved them. Allah's response lasted 309 years.

35

A believers' most powerful tool is his *dua*.

Imam Ibn al-Qayyim says regarding this رحمه الله: "If Allah did not want to accept your *dua*, He would have not guided you to make it (in the first place)."

He رحمه الله also said: "whoever is inspired (By Allah) to supplicate (to Allah), then a response has already been intended for him, for Allah has said 'Call on me, I will answer you' [Quran 40:60]."

36

The living heart

Ibn Qayyim رحمه الله said: “The keys to the life of the heart lie in:

1. Reflecting upon the Quran.
2. Being humble before Allah in secret.
3. Leaving sins.”

37

“And whatever you have of favor – it is from Allah.” [Quran 16:53]

Being content and thankful to Allah ﷻ for the innumerable blessings He has bestowed upon us is the key to a sound and happy heart; recognizing that whatever Allah ﷻ has bestowed upon us was never ours but was a gift in the first place that we were undeserving of.

Bakr b. ʿAbdullāh al-Muzanī رحمه الله, said: “O son of Adam, if you wish to know the magnitude of the blessings that Allah has bestowed upon you then close your eyes.”

38

The light of guidance Muhammad ﷺ said: "Whoever among you wakes up physically healthy, feeling safe and secure within himself, with food for the day, it is as if he has acquired the whole world."[1]

---

[1] Sunan Ibn Māja vol. 5, Book 37, Hadith 4141. Graded *ḥasan*.

39

Ibn al-Qayyim رحمه الله said: "If Allah wants well for a servant, he strips away from his heart the ability to see his own good deeds and to speak about them with his tongue, and preoccupies him with seeing his own sin and it continues to remain in front of his eyes until he enters Paradise."[1]

When preoccupied with one's self-development and spiritual growth, one continuously benefits from anything taking place in their life whether it is an apparent bad or good. When one is steadfast and patient, contentment and thankfulness will be present, leading to Allah ﷻ being pleased with His servant.

Ibn Taymiyyah رحمه الله said: "I have realized that the best *dua* one can make is for Allah to be pleased with them."[2]

Ibn al-Jawzi رحمه الله said, regarding this: " You are the most precious creature to Allah, so be content with what Allah has decreed for you, because he who loves never questions or accuses the one he loves.

---

1 *Ṭarīq al-Hijratayn*, 1/168-169.
2 *Jāmiʿ al-Ādāb* 1/408.

The grace of Allah upon you in all that He has created for your sake is as clear as daylight; so how could you imagine that He would be neglectful when you are at the root of it all?"[1]

[1] Ibn al-Jawzi, *Seeds of Admonishment and Reform*.

40

For those who make Allah their primary concern, there is only peace, because whatever happens to them in this life is considered good and is accepted as the will of Allah. Imagine having only good in your life. That is the state of this type of believer, as the Prophet ﷺ says: "Wondrous are the believers' affairs. For him there is good in all his affairs, and this is so only for the believer. When something pleasing happens to him, he is grateful and that is good for him; and when something displeasing happens to him, he is enduring (has *ṣabr*), and that is good for him."[1]

[1] Ṣaḥīḥ Muslim 2999.

41

ʿAlī b. Abū Ṭālib رضي الله عنه said : "Allah does not inspire the seeking of forgiveness in any servant He wishes to punish."

Ibn al-Jawzi رحمه الله said: "Never become impatient if the hardship continues for long, and never tire of supplication. You are being tested by the hardship, and your patient and supplication are acts of worship, there never despair of God's mercy, even if it the hardship is long in duration."[1]

[1] Ikram Hawramani, *The Sayings of Ibn al-Jawzi.*

42

The Prophet ﷺ said: "Even if a person was in *sujūd* from birth until death, they will still be regretful on the Day of Judgment."[1]

This powerful hadith captures the urgent importance of doing goods no matter what they are. We need every good deed we can muster for the Day of the great gathering.

The Quran mentions the wise man Luqmān's advice to his son:

"We endowed Luqman with wisdom: 'Be thankful to God: whoever gives thanks benefits his own soul, and as for those who are thankless—God is self-sufficient, worthy of all praise.

Luqman counselled his son, 'My son, do not attribute any partners to God: attributing partners to Him is a terrible wrong.'

We have commanded people to be good to their parents: their mothers carried them, with strain upon strain, and it takes two years to wean them.

[1] *Ṣaḥīḥ al-Targhīb* vol. 3, p.424.

Give thanks to Me and to your parents– all will return to Me.

If they strive to make you associate with Me anything about which you have no knowledge, then do not obey them. Yet keep their company in this life according to what is right, and follow the path of those who turn to Me. You will all return to Me in the end, and I will tell you everything that you have done. [And Luqman continued], 'My son, if even the weight of a mustard seed were hidden in a rock or anywhere in the heavens or earth, God would bring it [to light], for He is all subtle and all aware. Keep up the prayer, my son; command what is right; forbid what is wrong; bear anything that happens to you steadfastly: these are things to be aspired to. Do not turn your nose up at people, nor walk about the place arrogantly, for God does not love arrogant or boastful people. Go at a moderate pace and lower your voice, for the ugliest of all voices is the braying of asses.'" [Quran 31:12-19]

43

Ibn 'Umar رضي الله عنه narrated:

"The Messenger of Allah ﷺ took hold of some part of my body and said: 'O 'Abdullāh, be in the world like a stranger or a passerby, and count yourself among the inhabitants of the grave.'"[1]

Ibn al-Qayyim رحمه الله said: "This world is like a shadow: run after it and you will never be able to catch it; turn your back against it and it has no choice but to follow you"

---

[1] Jāmiʿ al-Tirmidhī 2333. Graded *ṣaḥīḥ*.

44

"... and verily for everything a servant loses there is a substitute, but the one who loses Allah will never find anything to replace Him."[1]

Al-Ḥasan al-Baṣrī رحمه الله said: "O son of Adam, after Prophet Moses objected to [the actions of] Khidr on three occasions, the latter said, 'This is the parting between you and me'. Then how will it be with you, who disobey your Lord many times in a single day? Do you feel so secure (and sure) that He will not say to you, 'This is the parting between you and Me'?"[2]

---

[1] Ibn al-Qayyim, *al-Dā' wa-l-Dawā'*, faṣl 49.
[2] Aid al Qarni, *Don't be Sad*.

45

"Do not be afraid, I am with you." [Quran 20:46]

In moments of sadness Shaytan comes and wants you to let go of Allah ﷻ. Faith in Allah ﷻ does not take difficulty or sadness away, but it makes us strong enough to go through them without breaking.

Muṣʿab b. Saʿd narrated from his father that a man said:

"O Messenger of Allah ﷺ! Which of the people is tried most severely?" He said: "The Prophets, then those nearest to them, then those nearest to them. A man is tried according to his religion; if he is firm in his religion, then his trials are more severe, and if he is frail in his religion, then he is tried according to the strength of his religion. The servant shall continue to be tried until he is left walking upon the earth without any sins."[1]

[1] Jāmiʿ al-Tirmidhī 2398. Graded *ḥasan.*

46

Rābiʿa al-ʿAdawīya, may Allah be pleased with her, said: "He does not refuse sustenance to the one who speaks ill of Him. How then could He refuse sustenance to the one whose soul is overflowing with love for Him?"

ʿUmar said, "I heard the Messenger of Allah, may Allah bless him and grant him peace, say, 'If you were to rely on Allah as He should be relied on, He would provide for you as He provides for the birds. They go out early in the morning hungry and return in the evening full.'"[1]

Shaykh Ibn ʿUthaymīn رحمه الله explains this: **If you were to rely on Allah as He should be relied on** means: with a genuine reliance on Allah, the Great and Almighty, and with complete trust in Him with regards to seeking your sustenance and other things. **He would provide for you as He provides for the birds**: The sustenance of the birds is on Allah because the birds do not have an owner, hence, they fly wherever they please in the air. They leave early in the morning from their nests to obtain the sustenance of Allah. **They go out early**

[1] Jāmiʿ al-Tirmidhī 2344. Graded *ḥasan*.

in the morning hungry: There is nothing in their stomachs when they go out during the early part of the day, but they depend on their Lord Almighty **and return** meaning they return in the later part of the day **full** meaning with filled stomachs from the sustenance of Allah.

47

A Khutbah given by Nouman Ali Khan highlighted the balance in life and the outlook we should adopt.

In moments of sadness Shaytan comes and wants you to let go of Allah. Faith in Allah doesn't take difficulty or sadness away, but it makes us strong enough to go through them without breaking

Your connection with Allah is that of intimate and close friendship. You talk every day. It is a daily interaction, which is strong–it affects our emotions and way we think. For some of us Allah becomes a distant concept. It should be deep and intimate. Benefit of 5 prayers: conversation.

Humans were created in difficulty: exhaustive labor: emotional, health-wise, physical, financially, because of people as life is designed with difficulty. Because we are believers doesn't mean our problems disappear.

Allah created us in a storm, worried about sinking—faith gives you the strength and ability to navigate and go through the storm.

Two of the hardest burdens: sadness (the past - feeling sad is not a sign of not having faith – think of

Ya'qūb عليه السلام and our Prophet ﷺ regarding Khadijah) and fear (worrying about the future). Think of the mother of Mūsā عليه السلام: she was told to throw her child in the water. He may flip, may sink etc. Allah told her not to be sad or afraid. Allah helps you navigate these feelings and allows you to stay sane through them. You and I are not capable of controlling our emotions without Allah. Strength is given by Allah to go through these emotions.

The word "rabb" (Lord) firstly gives the meaning of the One who keeps making this easy and gives constantly more than I deserve. Secondly, He makes sure always for me to grow out of weakness and sadness. The One who makes sure I don't fall apart and stay in place. Thirdly, He is in charge of what I do. When this view is adopted, the power that the creation has over you bounces off of you and goes away. Reality does not change but you change. You keep struggling to straighten yourself.

48

Ibn al-Qayyim رحمه الله said: "Be in this worldly life like a bee, when it eats, it eats what is pure (i.e. nectar); when it feeds, it feeds what is pure (i.e. honey). And when it lands on something, it does not break it nor cause it ruin."

Narrated Abū Hurayra رضي الله عنه:

Allah's Messenger ﷺ said, "The example of a believer is that of a fresh green plant the leaves of which move in whatever direction the wind forces them to move and when the wind becomes still, it stand straight. Such is the similitude of the believer: He is disturbed by calamities (but is like the fresh plant he regains his normal state soon). And the example of a disbeliever is that of a pine tree (which remains) hard and straight till Allah cuts it down when He will."[1]

[1] Ṣaḥīḥ al-Bukhārī 7466.

49

ʿAlī b. Abū Ṭālib رضي الله عنه said: "I will be patient even until my patience tires of my patience."

The patient have unlimited and infinite reward from Allah ﷻ Himself.

"Surely, Allah is with those who are *al-ṣābirūn* (the patient ones)" [Quran 8:46]

"But if you remain patient and become *al-muttaqūn* (the pious ones), not the least harm will their cunning do to you. Surely, Allah surrounds all that they do" [Quran 3:120]

"Only those who are patient shall receive their rewards in full, without reckoning." [Quran 39:10]

"And Allah loves *al-ṣābirūn* (the patient ones)" [Quran 3:146]

Abu Hurayra رضي الله عنه reported:

The Prophet ﷺ said, "When Allah loves a servant, He calls out to Jibril and says: 'I love so-and-so; so love him'. Then Jibril loves him. After that he (Jibril) announces to the inhabitants of heavens that Allah loves so- and-so; so love him; and the inhabitants of the heavens (the angels) also love him and then make people on earth love him."[1]

[1] Ṣaḥīḥ al-Bukhārī 7485. Ṣaḥīḥ Muslim 2637 a.

50

Hope for the believer–are there any words more comforting to the soul than these?

Anas رضي الله عنه said that he heard the Messenger of Allah ﷺ say: "O son of Adam! Verily as long as you called upon Me and hoped in Me, I forgave you, despite whatever may have occurred from you, and I did not mind. O son of Adam! Were your sins to reach the clouds of the sky, then you sought forgiveness from Me, I would forgive you, and I would not mind. So son of Adam! If you came to me with sins nearly as great as the earth, and then you met Me not associating anything with Me, I would come to you with forgiveness nearly as great as it."[1]

[1] Jāmiʿ al-Tirmidhī 3540. Graded *ḥasan*.

51

Ibn 'Abbās رضي الله عنه narrated:

"I was behind the Prophet ﷺ one day when he said: 'O boy! I will teach you a statement: Be mindful of Allah and He will protect you. Be mindful of Allah and you will find Him before you. When you ask, ask Allah, and when you seek aid, seek Allah's aid. Know that if the entire creation were to gather together to do something to benefit you- you would never get any benefit except that Allah had written for you. And if they were to gather to do something to harm you- you would never be harmed except that Allah had written for you. The pens are lifted, and the pages are dried.'"[1]

[1] Jāmiʿ al-Tirmidhī vol. 4, Book 11, Hadith 2516. Graded *ḥasan*.

52

Ibn al-Jawzi رحمه الله said: "So be like Mūsā عليه السلام and do not abandon your self-discipline until you arrive at the meeting point of the two oceans. Stand on the leg of patience (praying all night) even if standing is too wearisome, as it is better than sitting down. O you who has been asleep all night long, the company has already left, and the sun of old-age is upon you and yet your sleep does not end."[1]

---

[1] *Kitāb al-Laṭā'if fī-l-Wa'ẓ.*

53

"To whomever, male or female, does good deeds and has faith, We shall give a good life and reward them according to the best of their actions." [Quran 16:97]

Ibn al-Jawzi رحمه الله said: "you have known the story of Prophet Yūnus -عليه السلام- when he had previous righteous deeds that enabled his release from the trial he suffered."[1]

Allah ﷻ said regarding this: "If he had not been one of those who glorified God often, he would have stayed in its belly until the Day when all are raised up." [Quran 37:143-144]

[1] *Disciplining the Soul.*

54

Ibn al-Jawzi رحمه الله said: "the most precious thing in this world is knowing Allah."[1]

Knowing Allah ﷻ entails knowing what He has promised us and the perfection of His words, actions and attributes. Knowing these will allow us to put forth correct worship, trust and hope in Allah ﷻ.

A poet[2] once said:

"I said to the almond tree,

'Friend, speak to me of God'

And the almond tree blossomed."

A wise person said: "live in such a way that those who know you but do not know God will come to know God because they know you."

---

[1] *Captured Thoughts*, p.643.
[2] Nikos Kazantzakis.

55

Ibn al-Jawzi رحمه الله wrote: "At all times, strive for that which will benefit you, seek the help of Allah, and do not be helpless. If anything (bad) befalls you, do not say, 'if only I had done such-and-such, then such-and-such would have happened.' Rather you should say, 'Allah preordained this, and whatever He will He does,' for the words 'if only' open the door to Satan." [1]

---

[1] Ibn al-Jawzi, *Disciplining the Soul.*

56

Ibn al-Qayyim رحمه الله said: "From the perfection of Allah's *iḥsān* (goodness and bounty) is that He allows His servant to taste the bitterness of the break before the sweetness of the mend. So He does not break his believing servant except to mend him. And He does not withhold from him, except to give him. And He does not test (with hardship), except to cure him."[1]

My suffering became easier because my Lord promised me ease, not once, but twice: "So truly where there is hardship there is also ease; truly where there is hardship there is also ease." [Quran 94:5-6]

---

[1] Ibn al-Qayyim, *Mukhtaṣar al-Ṣawāʿiq al-Mursala ʿalā al-Jahmīya wa-l-Muʿaṭṭila.*

57

"Treat people as you want Allah to treat you on the Day of Judgment."[1]

A wise person said: "Suppose I can endure Your punishment (of the fire) but how will I endure my separation from You (my Lord)!"

---

[1] Yasmin Mogahed.

58

"The beauty of our religion is that the reward is dependent on the sincerity of our trying and not in the attainment of the results."[1]

ʿUmar b. al-Khaṭṭāb رضي الله عنه reported the Messenger of Allah ﷺ as saying "Actions are to be judged only by intentions and a man will have only what he intended."[2]

[1] Yasir Qadhi.
[2] Sunan Abī Dawūd 2201. Graded *ṣaḥīḥ*.

59

The key to happiness is to always be thankful for what you have. Always thank Allah. Always praise Allah. Always talk to Allah. The One who created you understands you best. Do not worry, Allah will grant all of your prayers; He knows what is best for you, which places are best for you and which people are best for you and knows the best time for these blessings to come in your life. The key to happiness is to always be thankful and content with Allah's decrees.

"When you are going through something hard and you start wondering where Allah is. Remember, the teacher is always quiet during a test."[1]

---

[1] Nouman Ali Khan.

60

Yasmin Mogahed's words highlight the right mindset: "Imagine that you're shopping with someone you love. No, not just someone you love. Someone you're madly in love with. Now suppose that this person picks out a gift for you in a particular color and style. How would you feel about that gift? Chances are you'll cherish it simply because of who gave it to you, simply because of who picked it out for you. There are things, events, people in your life that Allah has picked out for you. Are you pleased with His choice? Do we not love the gift simply because of who picked it out? You will know you really love someone, when you love anything that comes from them—no matter what it is. And you will love their gift, not for any quality in the gift itself—but only for who it came from."

Yaḥyā b. Muʿādh رحمه الله said: "The whole world from its beginning until its end is not worth an hour of sadness, so what about the sadness of a whole life?"[1]

---

[1] Jamāl al-Dīn Abū Bakr Khuwārizmī, *Kitāb Mufīd al-ʿUlūm wa-Mubīd al-Humūm.*

61

If Shaytan looks at you and sees that you are consistent in an act of obedience to Allah, he will try to come to you again and again. If he sees that you are persistent in your actions (despite his efforts) he will tire of you and leave you. But if he sees that you are one day like this one day like that, he will have high hopes in you.

"He promises them and entices them; what the devil promises is no more than an illusion." [Quran 4:120]

"O you who believe, you shall embrace total submission; do not follow the steps of Satan, for he is your most ardent enemy." [Quran 2:208]

The words of al-Ḥasan al-Baṣrī رحمه الله have much wisdom behind them, contemplating them allows us to realize our internal state of affairs and to rectify ourselves so as to fall within these verses:

"As for My servants, you have no power over them." Your Lord suffices as an advocate [Quran 17:65]

"Except those among Your worshipers who are devoted absolutely to You alone." He said, "This is a law that is inviolable. "You have no power over My servants. You only have power over the strayers who follow you." [Quran 15:40-42]

"He has no power over those who believe and trust in their Lord. His power is limited to those who choose him as their master, those who choose him as their god." [Quran 16:99-100]

"He said, 'I swear by Your majesty, that I will send them all astray. Except Your worshipers who are devoted absolutely to You alone.'" [Quran 38:82-83]

62

From the wise sayings of Luqmān:

"If you are in a prayer, then take care of your heart; if you are eating, then take care of your throat; if you are in another man's house, then take care of your eyes; if you are among people, then take care of your tongue. Remember two matters and forget two matters: remember Allah and death; forget any good you have done to another and any evil that was done to you by another."[1]

[1] Abdul-Malik Mujahid, *Gems and Jewels*, p.190.

63

Ibn al-Qayyim رحمه الله said: "Worship and obedience illuminate the heart and make it strong and steadfast, until it becomes like a clear mirror, shining with light. When Shaytan draws close, he is struck by its light like those who try to eavesdrop (in the heavens) are struck by the shooting stars, and Shaytan flees from this heart with more terror than a wolf fleeing from a lion."

Shaykh al-Islām Ibn Taymiyyah رحمه الله said: "She soul? It will not find relief in this world except by remembering Allah"

64

The Prophet ﷺ said, "Verily your Lord is Generous and Shy. If His servant raises his hands to Him (in supplication) He becomes shy to return them empty."[1]

'Umar b. al-Khaṭṭāb رضي الله عنه said, "I do not have any anxiety about the answer, but I worry about the *dua* itself, because anyone who is inspired by Allah to make *dua* immediately invokes His response when he makes the *dua*."[2]

[1] Sunan Abī Dawūd 1488. Graded ṣaḥīḥ.
[2] Ibn Taymiyyah, *Majmū'at al-Fatāwā* vol. 8.

65

Five reasons why Allah ﷻ puts us through trials:

1. To direct you (He wants us to always return to Him).
2. To inspect you (to test your faith).
3. To protect you (from misguidance).
4. To correct you (from your sins and straying).
5. To perfect you.

66

Ibn al-Jawzi رحمه الله said: "If you want to know your value with your Lord, look to how He is using you and what actions he has kept you busy with."

As a doer of good one not only finds tranquility from within, but also spreads this tranquility passively to those around oneself. This emanates from performing actions that Allah ﷻ has prescribed and avoiding ones that He has prohibited. While preforming such acts, one is inclined to thank Allah ﷻ for guiding to such noble endeavor in turn leading to gratefulness which not only means contentment but also happiness.

67

Don't compare your life to others,
There is no comparison between the sun and the moon;
They shine when it is their time.

Sahl b. Saʿd رضي الله عنه narrated that the Messenger of Allah ﷺ said:

"If the world to Allah was equal to a mosquito's wing, then He would not allow the disbeliever to have a sip of water from it."[1]

[1] Sunan Ibn Māja Vol. 5, Book 37, Hadith 4110. Graded *ḥasan*.

68

The Prophet ﷺ sought refuge in Allah ﷻ from sadness: "O Allah! I seek refuge with You from worry and sadness, from incapacity and laziness, from cowardice and miserliness, from being heavily in debt and from being overpowered by (other) men."[1]
Ibn al-Qayyim رحمه الله said: "Sadness weakens the heart and diminishes determination and wanting to go forward. And there is nothing more beloved to Shaytan than the sadness of a believer."

Ibn al-Qayyim رحمه الله said: "Do not ruin your happiness with worry, and do not ruin your mind with pessimism. Do not ruin your success with deception and do not ruin the optimism of others by destroying it. Do not ruin your day by looking back at yesterday. If you think about your situation, you will find that Allah ﷻ has given you things without asking, so have trust in Allah ﷻ that He does not prevent anything you want except there is goodness in it for you. You could be sleeping, and the doors of the heavens are being opened with *duas* being made on your behalf, subḥanAllāh: perhaps from someone poor whom you helped, or

[1] Ṣaḥīḥ al-Bukhārī 6369.

someone sad whom you brought joy, or someone passing by and you smiled at him, or someone in distress and you removed it. So do not ever underestimate any good deeds."

One of the righteous predecessors said: "I make *dua* to Allah ﷻ for something I want, and if He gives it to me then I am happy once and if He does not give it to me then I am happy ten times because the first was my choice and the second was Allah's choice."

Al-Saʿdī رحمه الله said: "Life is short so do not shorten it with worries, grief, and sadness."

69

Ibn ʿUthaymīn رحمه الله said: "If you truly contemplated the meaning of *Allāhu akbar* (in *ṣalāh*), the world would vanish from your thoughts. This is because Allah is greater than everything, and you are standing before the One greater than everything."

"The *ṣalāh* should be seen as an honor and a gift rather than a burden to be performed and get done with."[1] The honor we are presented with five times a day, not once or twice or three times but five times a day to stand before the Lord of the worlds is the epitome of honor and blessedness that we can experience in our day.

---

[1] Mufti Menk.

70

Ibn al-Qayyim رحمه الله said: "A person should spend an hour before bed for Allah, giving an account of his soul: what loss he suffered today and what income he gained today. Then he should renew repentance in front of Allah and fall asleep in the state of repentance. This should be done every night."[1]

Repentance is among the key heart softeners a servant of Allah can resort to when softening their heart and remaking their lives for the better. Sadness and loneliness in the heart is often a direct consequence of the sins a person commits. Remembering Allah, the hereafter, and death are impediments to sinning.

Imam al-Shāfiʿī رحمه الله remarked: "There is a verse in the Quran that every wrongdoer should be terrified of."

He was asked, "which verse is that?"

He replied: "And your Lord never forgets." [Quran 19:64]

---

[1] *Sharḥ Kitāb al-Tawḥīd.*

71

Anas narrated that the Messenger of Allah ﷺ said:

"When Allah wants good for his servant, He hastens his punishment in the world. And when He wants bad for His servant, He withholds his sins from him until he appears before Him on the Day of Judgment."

And with this (same) chain, (it was reported) from the Prophet ﷺ who said: "Indeed greater reward comes with greater trial. And indeed, when Allah loves a people He subjects them to trials, so whoever is content, then for him is pleasure, and whoever is discontent, then for him is wrath."[1]

---

[1] Jāmiʿ al-Tirmidhī 2396.

72

Abu Hafsah Abdul Malik Clare, may Allah reward him, said: "Don't wait to get old to worship Allah. If today is your last day, you are old already."

Imam Sufyān al-Thawrī رحمه الله said: "I fear that my *imān* will be taken away at the point of death."[1]

---

[1] *Jāmiʿ al-ʿUlūm wa-l-Ḥikma*, p.116.

73

Ibn al-Jawzi رحمه الله said: "Know that if people are impressed with you, in reality they are impressed with the beauty of Allah's covering of your sins."

He also said: "If you find darkness in your heart after you have sinned, then know that in your heart there is light, because of that light you felt the darkness."

74

Ibn Taymiyyah رحمه الله said: "If a person repents, Allah will love him and he will rise in status by virtue of his repentance."[1]

Ibn al-Jawzi رحمه الله said: "When you sigh, giving out breaths of regret, they rise and form clouds, to patter upon you drops of forgiveness. And if you shed a tear on the cheek of repentance, you will give life to your barren heart."[2]

---

[1] *Majmūʿ al-Fatāwā*, vol.10, p.45.
[2] *Kitāb al-Laṭāʾif fī-l-Waʿẓ*, p.152

75

Ibn al-Jawzi رحمه الله said: "One who fears Allah should know that Allah, glory to Him, is sufficient. He must not attach his heart to worldly means, for He says, glory be to Him, 'whosoever relies on Allah, He is sufficient for him.'"

"The amazing thing about putting trust in God is when you are standing at the cliff and He tells you to jump, it is not so you will fall. It is so He can make you fly."[1]

[1] Yasmin Mogahed.

76

Imam al-Shāfiʿī رحمه الله said: "No sadness lasts forever, nor any felicity nor any state of poverty or one of luxury. If you are the owner of a heart that is content, then you and owner of the world are equivalent."[1]

Ibn al-Jawzi رحمه الله said: "It is necessary for us to suffer good and bad. The good necessitates that we show thankfulness and the bad that we supplicate. If our supplication is not answered, this mean that it is intended that the test should finish, and for one to humbly submit to the decree.

This is where true faith shows itself. It is in submission and acceptance that the gems among men become apparent."[2]

---

[1] Ḥusayn ʿAbd Allāh Bāsalāmah, *Kitāb al-Jawāhir al-Limāʿ fī-mā Thabata bi-l-Samāʿ*.
[2] Ikram Hawramani, *The Sayings of Ibn al-Jawzi.*

77

Al-Ḥasan al-Baṣrī رحمه الله said "The intelligent man has his tongue behind his heart. If he intends to say something, he consults his heart whether he should say it or stay silent. The foolish man has his tongue in front of his heart. If he intends to say something, he lets his tongue speak first."[1]

Ibn al-Jawzi رحمه الله said: "By the amount that you honor God, glory to Him, He will honor you, and by the amount that you magnify His greatness in your esteem and increase your respect for Him, He will magnify your status and the respect you receive."

---

[1] *Shuʿab al-Īmān* 4366.

78

The Prophet ﷺ said:

"Indeed Allah extends His hand in the night to forgive the one who sins in the day, and He extends His hand in the day to forgive the one who sins at night, and this continues until the sun rises from the west."[1]

"O my servants, verily you sin by day and night, and I forgive all sins; so seek forgiveness from Me, and I will forgive you."[2]

"By the one Who has my soul in His hand, if you were not to sin, then Allah would remove you, and would bring another nation who sins, and who then seek forgiveness from Allah; and He would forgive them."[3]

---

[1] Ṣaḥīḥ Muslim 2759 a, b
[2] Ṣaḥīḥ Muslim 2577 a
[3] Ṣaḥīḥ Muslim 2748 a

79

Ibn al-Jawzi رحمه الله said: "(The one who follows the Quran and the Sunnah) will not live a life of suffering. This is illustrated by His saying, glory to Him: 'whosoever fears God, God will create for him a way out [Quran 65:2]'. If you see them suffer, then surely there is for them in recompense that which will turn any bitter drink into honey."

Mālik b. Dinār رحمه الله said: "Indeed, the Qur'an is the life of the heart, just as the rain is to the earth."

80

Bishr b. Ḥārith رحمه الله said: “You will not find the sweetness of worship until you place between you and your ego’s desires a barrier of steel”[1]

Isḥāq al-Mawṣlī said that (the caliph) al-Muʿtaṣim said to him, “O Isḥāq, if the ego’s desires overcome you, sound opinion will depart from you.”[2]

Imam al-Ghazali رحمه الله said: “Never have I dealt with anything more difficult than my own soul, which sometimes helps me and sometimes opposes me.”

---

[1] Ikram Hawramani, *The Sayings of Ibn al-Jawzi.*
[2] Ibid.

81

The Prophet ﷺ said:

"And know that what has befallen you was not going to miss you, and that which missed you was not meant to befall you."[1]

---

[1] Sunan Abī Dawūd 4700. Graded *ṣaḥīḥ*.

82

Ibn al-Qayyim رحمه الله: "Sins cause a great loneliness in the heart, so the sinner feels alone, away from his Lord, from people and even from his own soul! And the more his sins increase, the more his loneliness increases!"

"O you who spends his lifetime in disobeying his Lord! No one amongst your enemies is wicked to you than you are to yourself."[1]

[1] Ibn al-Qayyim, *al-Fawā'id*, p.107.

83

Dr. Mustafa Mahmud said: "Your vehicle to God is your prayer mat. The only safe spot on this ruined earth is the prayer mat."

Ibn al-Jawzi رحمه الله said: "What a pity! If they (those poor souls who indulge in the pleasures of this life and stay far from Allah, glory be to Him) were to truly know whom they had detached themselves from, they would prefer to be torn apart (out of regret)."[1]

[1] Kitāb al-Laṭā'if fī-l-Waʿẓ, p.102.

84

Yahya bin Mu'adh رحمه الله said: "the world is worthless to its Lord, and yet it belongs to Him. So it is not right that you value it so much and it is not even yours."

85

Dr. Mustafa Mahmud said: “It is almost a rule that the heart does not mend except through pain, and does not recover and regain its tenderness except through suffering.”

Ibn ‘Aṭā’ Allāh al-Iskandarī رحمه الله said: “Nothing is difficult if you seek it through your Lord, and nothing is easy if you seek it through yourself.”

86

Ibn al-Jawzi رحمه الله said: "Understand that life has occasions. One time it is poverty, and another time it is wealth. Once it is honor, and another it is humiliation. Happy is he who remains grounded in each situation."[1]

A wise man said: "Millions of souls in the darkness and Allah chose yours to be guided in His mercy."

---

[1] *Ṣayd al-Khāṭir.*

87

A wise man said: "some souls are so beautiful that their presence alone reminds you of God."

These are the types of friends we should be seeking.

Abū Hurayra رضي الله عنه reported:

"I heard the Prophet ﷺ saying, 'Man follows his friend's religion, you should be careful who you take for friends.'"[1]

It is reported that 'Umar b. al-Khaṭṭāb رضي الله عنه said: "Do not expose yourself to what does not concern you, stay away from your enemy, beware of [taking as] your friend anyone except the trustworthy amongst people—and there is no one who is trustworthy except one who fears Allah; and do not accompany the sinner in case you learn his sinfulness, and do not let him know your secrets, and consult those who fear Allah for your affairs."

[1] Sunan Abī Dawūd 4833. Graded *ḥasan.*

88

When blessings turn into blight:

It is reported that al-Ḥasan al-Baṣrī رحمه الله said: "Verily, Allah lets (a person) enjoy a blessing for as long as He wills. But when He is no longer thanked for it, He turns it into a punishment."[1]

He also said: "People appear similar during times of ease. But when hardship and trials arrive, that is when their true nature becomes apparent."[2]

---

[1] Ibn Abī al-Dunyā, *Kitāb al-Shukr*, article 17.
[2] Ikram Hawramani, *The Sayings of Ibn al-Jawzi*.

89

Abu Hurayrah reports that the Prophet ﷺ said[1]:

"Al-taqwā is here," and he pointed to his chest three times.

The Successor Ṭalq b. Ḥabīb رحمه الله said upon being asked about *taqwā*,

"That you perform the obedience of Allah upon a light from Allah, hoping for the reward of Allah. And you abandon disobedience of Allah upon a light from Allah, fearing the punishment of Allah."

Ibn al-Qayyim رحمه الله commented on this saying: "This is the best that has been said concerning the definition of *taqwā* for indeed every action must have a beginning cause to it and an objective. An action can never be considered to be obedience and a cause to draw one closer to Allah until its point of commencement and cause are unadulterated faith, not habit, not base desires, not the wish for praise and position, nor other such things. Its objective must be the reward that lies with Allah and His good pleasure, this being the definition of *iḥtisāb*

[1] Ṣaḥīḥ Muslim 2564.

(the patience of those seeking the reward from Allah)."

90

Ibn al-Qayyim رحمه الله said: "The one who is truthful does not care about his status in the eyes of the creation."[1]

Ibn al-Jawzi رحمه الله said: "Whoever acts pious for the sake of the creation is in effect worshipping them, although he does not realize it."

Clinging to the truth as if for dear life should also reflect our reality when we declare our testimony of faith. Guidance and faith are like water for fish. Without them, we cannot survive. Thus, sticking to the truth sincerely for the sake of Allah ﷻ will give us life and hope.

---

[1] *Madārij al-Sālikīn*, vol.2, p.289.

91

Ibn Rajab al-Ḥanbalī رحمه الله said: "Man! Were you to go to the door of the governor, he would not receive you or give you any attention, perhaps he will even prevent you from getting near him. But the King of Kings is saying, 'Whoever comes to Me walking, I will go to him running,' yet you turn away from Him and run after another! You have been cheated in the worst of manners and you have lost out in the severest of ways!"[1]

---

[1] Ibn Rajab al-Ḥanbalī, *The Journey to Allah*, p.68.

92

Ibn al-Jawzi رحمه الله said: "The planning of The Almighty is better for you than your own planning, and He could deprive you from what you ask to test your patient. So let Him see from you a determined patience and you will soon see from Him what will give you joy. And when you have cleaned the paths of answering from the stains of sins and were patient about what He has chosen for you, then everything that happens to you is better for you whether you were given or deprived of what you have requested."

93

Ibn Rajab al-Ḥanbalī رحمه الله said: "The worth of every man is judged by what he seeks. None can put a value to one who seeks Allah for this is immeasurable. The one who seeks after the world is too lowly to be valued. Al-Shiblī said, 'whoever holds fast to this world will be burned by its blaze until he becomes ashes blown about by the wind. Whoever holds on to the hereafter will be burned by its light such that he becomes a pure gold of the highest quality and is benefited from. Whoever holds on to Allah will be burned by the light of *tawḥīd* and will become a jewel that is beyond value'."

He also said: "Whoever's ambitions are truly great will only ever be content with seeking Allah, Glorious and Exalted is He."

94

Ibrāhīm b. Adham said: "We live such a life (of amazing pleasure in the worship of Allah) that if the kings knew about it, they would fight us over it with swords."

Ibn Taymiyyah رحمه الله said: "Sometimes the heart is in such a state that I say: if the people of paradise experience this, then they indeed have a wonderful life."

He also said: "The heart sometimes dances rapturously, from the happiness of remembering Allah and of feeling close to Him."

Aid al-Qarni said in his book: "Don't blindly feel grief; instead, make sure you know the value of the thing over which you feel sad."

95

Al-Bukhārī records on the authority of Abū Hurayra رضي الله عنه that the Prophet ﷺ said: "Your actions alone will not save any of you." They asked, "Messenger of Allah, not even you?" He replied, "Not even me, unless Allah were to envelop me in His mercy. Be firm; steadfast and balanced; and journey (worship) in the beginning of the day, the end of the day, and a portion of the latter part of the night (night prayers). Moderation, moderation! Through this will you attain your goal."[1]

He also recorded this hadith in another place with the wording[2]: "This religion is easy, none makes it hard upon himself except that it overwhelms him; therefore be firm, steadfast, and balanced; upon which have glad tidings! Seek help in this by journeying (to Allah) at the beginning of the day, at the end of the day, and a portion of the latter part of the night."[3]

---

[1] Ṣaḥīḥ al-Bukhārī 6463.
[2] Ibn Rajab al-Ḥanbalī, *The Journey to Allah*.
[3] Ṣaḥīḥ al-Bukhārī 39.

96

Aid al Qarni mentions in his book[1] six ingredients of happiness:

1. The first is to have a firm trust in Allah, the Almighty.
2. The second is resigning oneself to the inescapable fact that everything that is decreed will happen and will follow its unalterable course.
3. The third is that patience has no substitute for the positive effect it has on the afflicted.
4. The fourth is an unwavering belief in the implications of this question: "Without showing forbearance, what will I accomplish?"
5. The fifth is to ask oneself: "Why should I be a willful party to my own destruction?"
6. The sixth is knowing that from one hour to the next, circumstances are transformed, and difficulties vanish.

---

[1] Aid al Qarni, *Don't be Sad*.

97

Aid al Qarni lists yet another set of conclusions he reached after reading the biographies of successful people:

1. A person's value is based on the good he or she does. This is a saying of ʿAlī رضي الله عنه, and it means that a person's knowledge, character, worship and generosity are the yardsticks by which we measure his or her worth.

"Verily the most honorable of you with Allah is that (believer) who is pious." [Quran 49:13]

2. One's status in this life and in the hereafter depends on determination, striving, and sacrifice.

"And if they had intended to march out, certainly, they would made preparation for it..." [Quran 9:46]

"And strive hard in Allah's cause as you ought to strive (with sincerity and with all your efforts that His name should be superior." [Quran 22:78]

3. Each of us–by the will of Allah–is the maker of our own history. We write our life's story with our good and bad deeds.

"Indeed it is We Who bring the dead to life and record what they have put forth and what they have left behind, and all things We have enumerated in a clear register." [36:12]

4. Life is short and passes quickly. Do not make it shorter by sinning, by worrying, or by quarrelling.

"The day they see it, (it will be) as if they had not tarried (in the world) except an afternoon or a morning." [Quran 79:46]

98

Summarized from al-Dhahabī's *Siyar Aʿlām al-Nubalā'* (the biographies of renowned people)[1], is a central point:

Whoever places their hopes or trust in something or someone other than Allah, then Allah will abandon them and make that thing or person the cause of their ruin

"On the Day God will say, 'Call on those you claimed were My partners,' they will call them, but they will not answer; We shall set a deadly gulf between them. The evildoers will see the Fire and they will realize that they are about to fall into it: they will find no escape from it." [Quran 18:52-53]

"And verily, the devil hinder them from the path (of Allah), but they think that they are guided aright" [Quran 43:37]

---

[1] Aid al Qarni, *Don't be Sad.*

99

Imam al-Shāfiʿī رحمه الله said: "If you want to fix your heart, or would like to see improvement in your child or friend, or anyone for that matter, then direct them to places where the Quran is recited and direct them to be in the company of the Quran. Allah will then cause them to become better, regardless of whether they want to or not!"[1]

Shaykh al-Albānī رحمه الله said: "One proof is sufficient for the seeker of truth, but 1000 proofs are not enough for the person of desires."

Nouman Ali Khan, may Allah bless him, said: "Loyalty is to the truth, your loyalty is to the word of Allah, your loyalty is to where the evidence leads you."

---

[1] *Ḥilyat al-Awliyāʾ*, vol.9, p.123.

100

ʿUmar b. al-Khaṭṭāb رضي الله عنه said: "take account of yourselves before it is taken of you. Weigh your deeds before they are weighed for you (on the Day of Judgment), and beautify yourselves (with good deeds) for the great display (on the Day of Judgment).

"Know that pain comes with standing by the truth just like all the Prophets endured. Faith does not mean you will not have sadness, like Yaʿqūb عليه السلام was sad for having been separated from Yūsuf عليه السلام ; you cannot be reduced to a past mistake either just like Mūsā عليه السلام was not in regards for killing a man accidentally; people degrading you does not take away from Allah honoring you just like Maryam عليها السلام. These stories are live and forever relevant. Make an effort to ponder"[1]

---

[1] Nouman Ali Khan.

101

Al-Ḥasan al-Baṣrī رحمه الله says: "You will always find a believer questioning himself: 'What did I mean by this word? What did I eat this food for? What do I mean by speaking to myself thus?' A transgressor will go on never blaming himself."

The true believer is constantly self-reproaching as Allah ﷻ mentions in the Quran:

"And by the self-reproaching soul! Does man think We shall not put his bones back together? In fact, We can reshape his very fingertips." [Quran 75:2-4]

102

ʿUmar b. al-Khaṭṭāb رضي الله عنه said: "I am not worried about whether my *dua* will be responded to, but rather I am worried about whether I will be able to make *dua* or not. So if I have been guided (by Allah) to make *dua*, then (I know) that the response will come with it."[1]

"Reminders not advice:

1. You are strong enough to carry this trial or Allah would not have given it to you
2. He loves you more than anyone will ever love you including yourself
3. Maybe your pain is a blessing in ways only He knows, and you must trust
4. Ask Allah for healing but do not question His care for you
5. Your Duas are dearer to Him than those not tested like you

---

[1] *Al-Awayishah*, p.117.

103[1]

The nature of this world is that it's not perfect. That means we will at times go through pain, but not everyone goes through the process of healing.

From the start of our lives, we go through a process of pain in order to learn and grow. A baby must leave the comfort of the womb to enter this world. A toddler must learn to stand and fall, stand and fall, stand and fall, in order to walk.

When we get hurt, our focus is on our ego. We focus so much on our pain that we can't see outside of it, and in that state we stunt our own healing. One can understand why, but we end up making it worse for yourself, picking at the scab. However, it is important to state here that this does not delegitimize your pain and sadness. Our emotions are legitimate because they are created by Allah.

It is a dangerous statement to make that a believe should never be sad. The Prophets themselves felt sadness; in fact the day of Taif happened in the Year of Sadness! Allah does not ask us to suppress our

---

[1] Used with permission from The Sweetness of Healing by Yasmin Mogahed on www.VisionaireRamadan.com.

emotions because they serve a purpose. Yaʿqūb عليه السلام him lost Yūsuf عليه السلام and went blind out of sadness. This negates the myth that crying, and grief is from a lack of faith or patience. Rather, crying to Allah is the fastest way of healing. It is described in Quran as the state of *taḍarruʿ*—a state of humility and need for Allah. A believer will feel sad at times, but a believer should not despair. Despair and hopelessness is from Shaytan.

This is what faith (*imān*) does for a believer - it turns us to the power of *dua*. The core of *dua* is hope in Allah. One of the biggest mistakes we make in our *dua* is to restricting Allah. Allah's provision is endless, and nothing is impossible for Him. Zakarīyā عليه السلام learned from Maryam عليها السلام this important lesson. When he saw she received provision straight from Allah (fruits out of season), he asked Allah for a child even though he was old and his wife barren. Never limit the ability of Allah to provide for you. Never limit the mercy of Allah. When you ask, ask without restriction. The key to *dua* is hope. Never lose it.

104

A wise poet said: "my own soul that possess things is itself departing, so why should I cry over a possession when it leaves?"[1]

"Everything will perish save His face." [Quran 28:88]

"We have adorned the earth with attractive things so that We may test people to find out which of them do best, but We shall reduce all this to barren dust." [Quran 18:7-8]

[1] Aid al-Qarni, *Don't be Sad.*

105

Let Days Go Forth[1]

Let days go forth and do as they please

And remain firm when settled is the Decree

Don't be afraid of what happens by night

For the affairs of this world are not to last

And be a man, strong in the face of calamities

And let your nature be that of kindness and honesty

If your faults become too much in front of the people

And you wish that they were to be concealed,

Then know that kindness covers all faults

And how many faults are kept hidden by kindness!

No sadness lasts forever, nor any happiness

---

[1] Poem by Imam al-Shāfiʿī.

And you shall not remain in poverty, or any luxury

Generosity cannot be hoped from the miserly

For no water exists in the Fire for the thirsty

Your provision will not be lessened due to life's delays

And it cannot be increased due to your haste

If, in your heart, you possess contentment

Then you and those who possess the world are equal

And for him upon whose horizon death descends,

No earth can offer him protection, nor any sky

Indeed, the earth of Allah is certainly vast

But if decree descends, then decree is constricted

Let days be the ones that betray you at all times

For no cure can avail a person of death

106

Advice from Imam Ibn al-Qayyim رحمه الله:

"A friend will not (literally) share your struggles, and a loved one cannot physically take away your pain, and a close one will not stay up the night on your behalf. So look after yourself, protect yourself, nurture yourself and do not give life's events more than what they are really worth. Know for certain that when you break no one will heal you except you, and when you are defeated no one will give you victory except your determination. Your ability to stand up again and carry on is your responsibility. Do not look for your self-worth in the eyes of people; look for your worth from within your conscience. If your conscience is at peace then you will ascend high and if you truly know yourself then what is said about you will not harm you.

Do not carry the worries of this life because this is for Allah. And do not carry the worries of sustenance because it is from Allah. And do not carry anxiety for the future because it is in the Hands of Allah. Carry one thing: pleasing Allah. Because if you please Him, He pleases you, fulfills you and enriches you.

Do not weep from a life that made your heart weep. Just say, "Oh Allah compensate me with good in this life and the hereafter." Sadness departs with a *sajda*. Happiness comes with a sincere *dua*. Allah does not forget the good you do, nor does He forget the good you did to others and the pain you relieved them from. Nor will He forget the eye which was about to cry but you made it laugh.

Live your life with this principle: be good even if you do not receive good, not because for other's sake but because Allah loves those who do good."

107

The Prophet ﷺ said: "Indeed, the greatness of reward depends on the hardness of test. Indeed, if Allah loves certain people, He will test them. Whoever is pleased with the test will obtain His pleasure. Whoever detests it will obtain His detest."[1]

[1] Al-Tirmidhī 2396 and Ibn Māja 4031.

108

Imam Ibn al-Qayyim رحمه الله listed 10 ways of attaining Allah's love[1]:

1) Recitation of the Quran with reflection and with understanding of its meanings.

2) Seeking closeness to Allah by performing voluntary deeds after having performed obligatory ones, for that leads one to the highest levels of love.

3) Remembering Allah during every situation – with one's time, heart and deeds, one's share of that love is to the degree of one's share in that remembrance.

4) Preferring what He loves to what you love when your desires are strong.

5) Allowing your heart to reflect on His Names and Attributes.

6) Reflecting on His many favors and blessings, both the apparent ones and hidden ones, for that leads to His love.

---

[1] *Madārij al-Sālikīn.*

7) Having your heart softened as it is worshipping Allah.

8) Being alone with Him in worship when He descends during the last third of the night. And this means to invoke Him, to recite His Speech, to stand with all sincerity and with good manners and with good submission, and then to end that with repentance and with seeking His forgiveness.

9) Sitting with those who are truthful in their love of Allah.

10) Staying away from all that creates barriers between the heart and Allah.

109

Ibn al-Jawzi رحمه الله said in his writings: "Mālik b. Dīnār said, 'As much as you grieve for this world, the fear of the Day of Judgment leaves your heart.' Thus, as it is evident that sadness accompanies the heart of the righteous, excessive sadness therefore should be avoided. That is because one should feel sad regarding what he has missed, and I have already clarified the way to recant.

The best of the cures for sadness is to know that one cannot bring back what he has missed, rather by feeling sad he is adding another misfortune to the already existing misfortune ultimately making two misfortunes. A misfortune should not be made heavier by being saddened by it, rather it should be eased and pushed away. Ibn ʿAmr said, "If Allah takes something away from you, get busy with anything that will not make you think about it." In addition, what Allah gives you in place of what was taken away from you makes that easier. However, if there is nothing that can make the matter easier, then one should struggle to push away sadness from his heart.

Know that what calls to sorrow and sadness is *hawā* (the ego's propensities) not the mind, simply because the mind does not call to that which is not useful. One should know that the matter, eventually, will get easier after some time, therefore he should strive to bring forward that which is supposed to happen then (i.e. comfort) so that he relaxes during the time of difficulty until such ease and comfort is achieved. One of the things that make sorrow and sadness disappear is knowing that it is useless, believing in its reward and remembering those who are afflicted with worse misfortunes."[1]

---

[1] Ibn al-Jawzi, *Disciplining the Soul.*

110

Ibn al-Jawzi رحمه الله speaks of worry and sadness: "*Ghamm* (grief) occurs due to misfortunes that happened in the past while *hamm* (worry) occurs due to an expected misfortune in the future. When someone has the feeling of grief in regard to his past sins, his grief will benefit him, because he is rewarded for it. Whoever worries about a good deed he wishes to do; his worry will benefit him as well. However if someone grieves for something that he missed from this world, then [he should know] that the missed thing will not return and that grief harms, so practically he is adding harm to harm, as I have mentioned in the previous chapter.

A resolute person should protect himself from what brings about grief, and that is losing an object he loves. Therefore, whoever has many objects that he loves, his grief increases, and whoever decreases his objects of love his grief decreases accordingly. Someone may say, when I have no objects of love I also still have grief, we affirm this, but we say to him; your grief over not having a loved one is not even a tenth of the grief experienced by the one who has lost a loved one. Have you not noticed that the one who does not have a child lives in grief but not as much as the one who lost his child?

Moreover when a person becomes accustomed to what he loves and enjoys it for a long period of time, it takes over his heart, therefore when he loses it he will feel the bitterness of his loss which will be greater than all the satisfaction he had during his lifetime. This is because the loved one is corresponding to the self just as health corresponds to it, which causes the self not to find satisfaction except in it, for its absence disturbs it.

A poet said: "The prudent imagines in himself his tribulations before they befall him. If they suddenly befall him, they do not surprise him because he had already imagined them. And the ignorant trusts the days, and he forgets the demise of those who came before him."

This is why the self grieves for its loss much more than it rejoices in its presence, because the inner self believes that what it had was its given right to possess. Therefore a wise person should monitor the closeness between himself and his beloved to ensure it remains moderately balanced. However if he requires that which brings about grief (i.e. some object or person), then the cure is first to believe in predestination and that whatever Allah predestines is going to happen. He should then know that life is founded on distress, all constructed buildings shall eventually be ruined, all gatherings shall eventually depart, and whoever wants the lasting of what does not last is like he who wants what does not exist to exist. Therefore he should not ask of life what it was not created for.

A poet said: "It [the worldly life] is founded on distress yet you want it, free of harm and distress." One should imagine that what befell him is multiplied, for this is when what he suffers will be easier on him. It is a habit of smart porters to put something heavy on top of what they are carrying, and then after taking a few steps, to remove the heavy object as that makes what they are carrying feel lighter. One should also wait, in times of prosperity for an attack of tribulation, so that if any tribulation befalls him, he should think of what remains instead of what he has lost so that when part of that befalls him it becomes very easy on him. An example is when someone loses some money, so he counts what remains, and then considers the remaining as a profit. Or if someone imagines that he loses his eyesight, so that when he has ophthalmia, it becomes easy on him to bear this illness; likewise with other harmful matters."[1]

---

[1] Ibn al-Jawzi, *Disciplining the Soul.*

111

"The one who goes against his whims and desires, Shaytan flees from his shadow."[1]

On the other hand, the one who follows his whims and desires will feel a sense of humiliation, indignity, worthlessness and insignificance, which is the punishment that Allah has decreed for those who disobey Him as al-Ḥasan رحمه الله said: "Even if they ride the finest of mounts, the effect of sin will never depart from them. Allah insists that the one who disobeys Him will be humiliated."

Allah, may He be glorified and exalted, has connected strength to obedience to Him, and humiliation to disobedience to Him. Allah says:

"But honor, power and glory belong to Allah, and to His Messenger ﷺ and to the believers."

---

[1] Ibn al-Qayyim, *One Hundred Pieces of Advice.*